Song of La Selva

A Story of a Costa Rican Rain Forest

The
Nature
Conservancy®

For my grandsons, Dakota and Anthony — J.B.

This book is dedicated to my sister, Fareedah (Rita) Muhammad,
an animal lover who always hated frogs. But this one is beautiful,
strong, and a survivor, just like she is — H.B.

Book copyright © 1998 Trudy Corporation, 353 Main Avenue, Norwalk, CT 06851.

Soundprints is a division of Trudy Corporation, Norwalk, Connecticut.

Book layout: Diane Hinze Kanzler
Editor: Judy Gitenstein

First Edition 1998
10 9 8 7 6 5 4 3 2
Printed in Hong Kong

Acknowledgments:
   Our very special thanks to Dr. Maureen A. Donnelly from Florida International
University's Department of Biological Sciences for her curatorial review.

Library of Congress Cataloging-in-Publication Data

Banks, Joan.
   Song of La Selva: a story of a Costa Rican rain forest / by Joan Banks;
   illustrated by Higgins Bond.
         p.   cm.
   Summary: A strawberry poison dart frog travels through a Costa Rican rain forest
   searching for his territory.
         ISBN 1-56899-586-5 (hardcover)   ISBN 1-56899-587-3 (pbk.)
   1. Strawberry poison frog — Juvenile fiction.   [1. Poison frogs — Fiction.
   2. Frogs — Fiction.   3. Rain forests — Fiction.   4. Costa Rica — Fiction.]
   I. Higgins Bond, ill.   II. Title.
         PZ10.3.B2153He   1998   98-13023
         [E] — dc21   CIP
                                                                                   AC

Song of La Selva

A Story of a Costa Rican Rain Forest

by Joan Banks

Illustrated by Higgins Bond

Soundprints™
Where Children Discover...

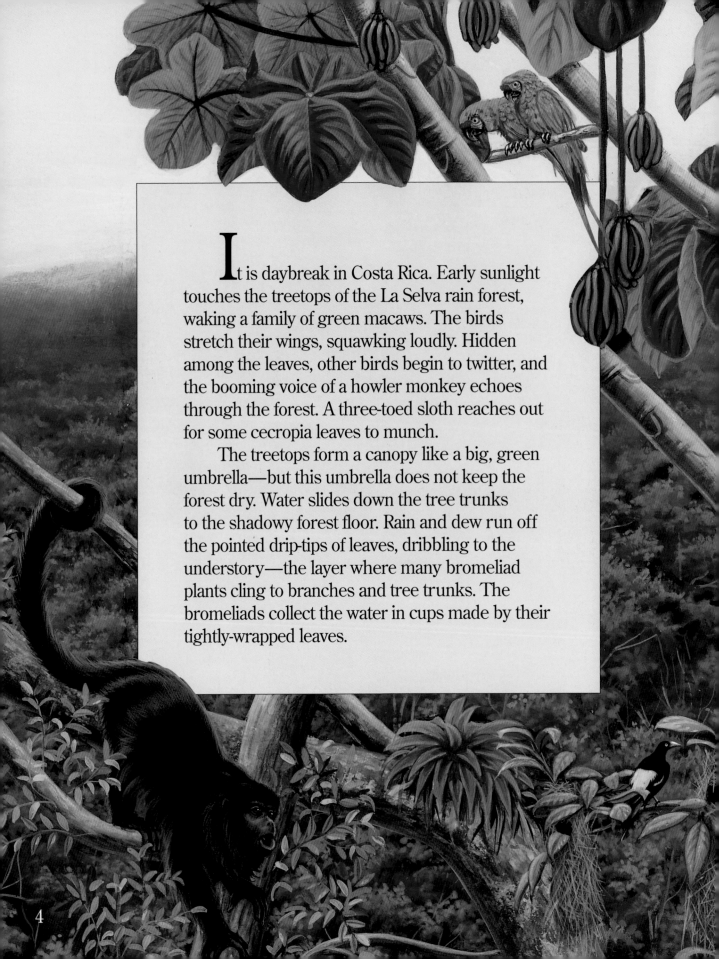

It is daybreak in Costa Rica. Early sunlight touches the treetops of the La Selva rain forest, waking a family of green macaws. The birds stretch their wings, squawking loudly. Hidden among the leaves, other birds begin to twitter, and the booming voice of a howler monkey echoes through the forest. A three-toed sloth reaches out for some cecropia leaves to munch.

The treetops form a canopy like a big, green umbrella—but this umbrella does not keep the forest dry. Water slides down the tree trunks to the shadowy forest floor. Rain and dew run off the pointed drip-tips of leaves, dribbling to the understory—the layer where many bromeliad plants cling to branches and tree trunks. The bromeliads collect the water in cups made by their tightly-wrapped leaves.

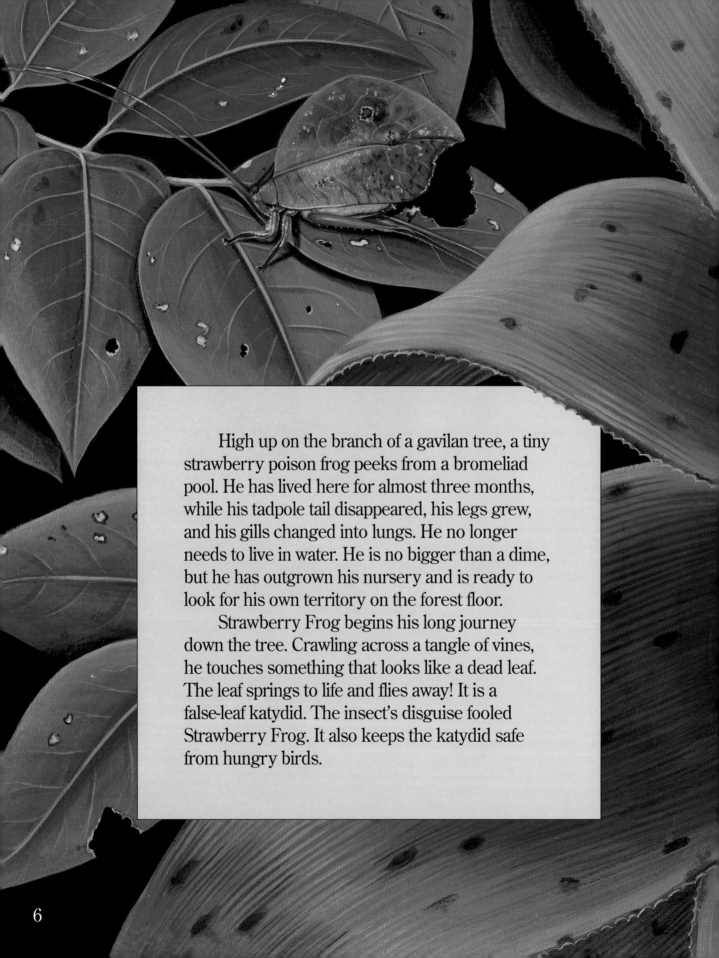

High up on the branch of a gavilan tree, a tiny strawberry poison frog peeks from a bromeliad pool. He has lived here for almost three months, while his tadpole tail disappeared, his legs grew, and his gills changed into lungs. He no longer needs to live in water. He is no bigger than a dime, but he has outgrown his nursery and is ready to look for his own territory on the forest floor.

Strawberry Frog begins his long journey down the tree. Crawling across a tangle of vines, he touches something that looks like a dead leaf. The leaf springs to life and flies away! It is a false-leaf katydid. The insect's disguise fooled Strawberry Frog. It also keeps the katydid safe from hungry birds.

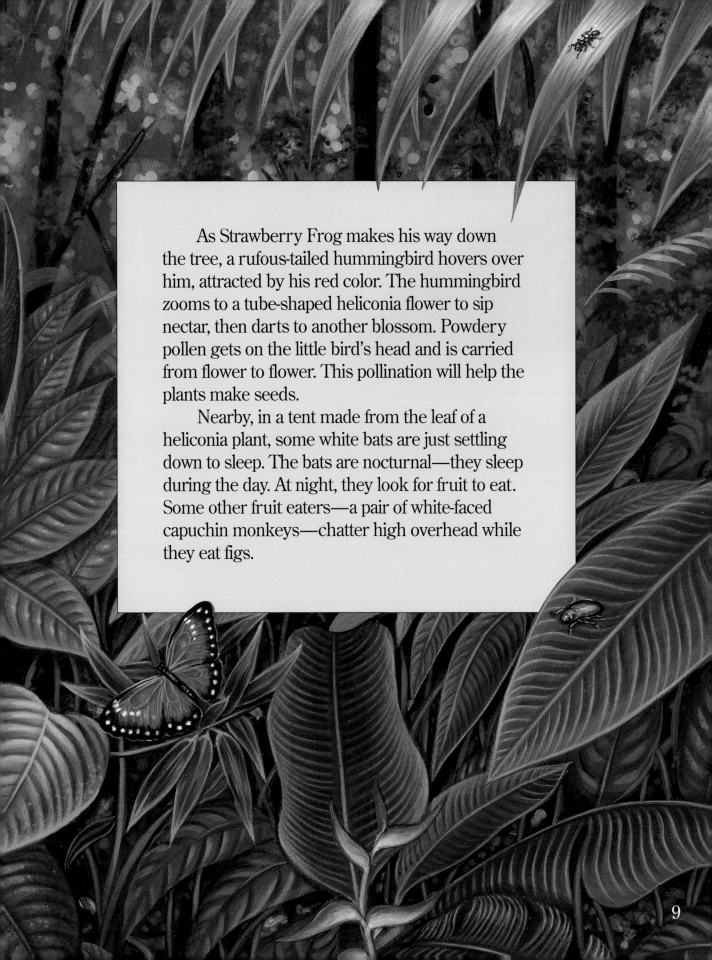

As Strawberry Frog makes his way down the tree, a rufous-tailed hummingbird hovers over him, attracted by his red color. The hummingbird zooms to a tube-shaped heliconia flower to sip nectar, then darts to another blossom. Powdery pollen gets on the little bird's head and is carried from flower to flower. This pollination will help the plants make seeds.

Nearby, in a tent made from the leaf of a heliconia plant, some white bats are just settling down to sleep. The bats are nocturnal—they sleep during the day. At night, they look for fruit to eat. Some other fruit eaters—a pair of white-faced capuchin monkeys—chatter high overhead while they eat figs.

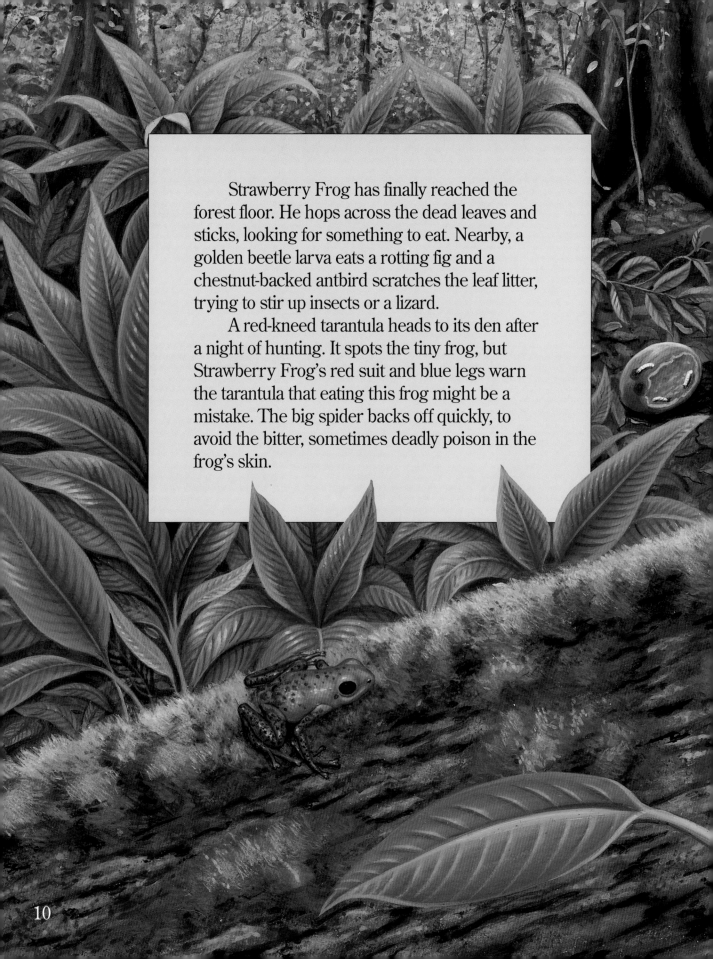

Strawberry Frog has finally reached the forest floor. He hops across the dead leaves and sticks, looking for something to eat. Nearby, a golden beetle larva eats a rotting fig and a chestnut-backed antbird scratches the leaf litter, trying to stir up insects or a lizard.

A red-kneed tarantula heads to its den after a night of hunting. It spots the tiny frog, but Strawberry Frog's red suit and blue legs warn the tarantula that eating this frog might be a mistake. The big spider backs off quickly, to avoid the bitter, sometimes deadly poison in the frog's skin.

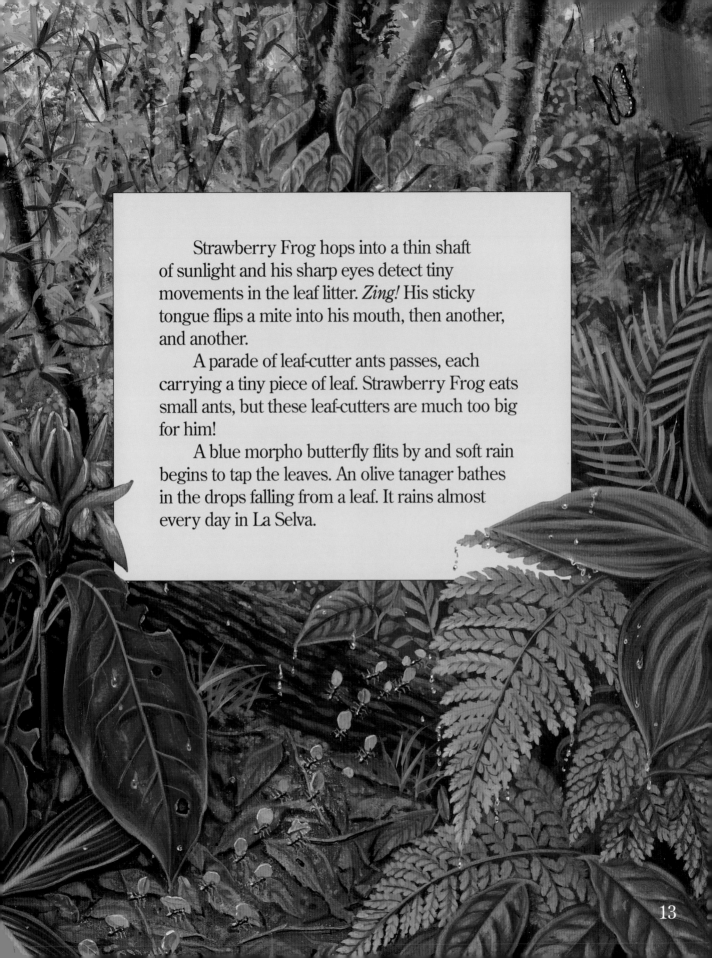

Strawberry Frog hops into a thin shaft of sunlight and his sharp eyes detect tiny movements in the leaf litter. *Zing!* His sticky tongue flips a mite into his mouth, then another, and another.

A parade of leaf-cutter ants passes, each carrying a tiny piece of leaf. Strawberry Frog eats small ants, but these leaf-cutters are much too big for him!

A blue morpho butterfly flits by and soft rain begins to tap the leaves. An olive tanager bathes in the drops falling from a leaf. It rains almost every day in La Selva.

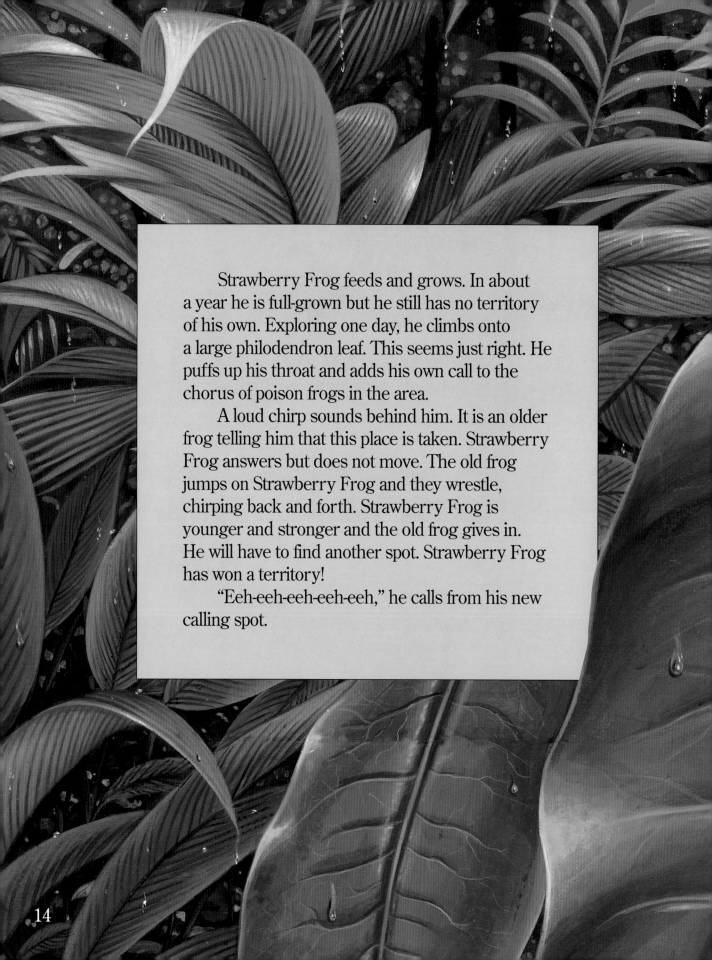

Strawberry Frog feeds and grows. In about a year he is full-grown but he still has no territory of his own. Exploring one day, he climbs onto a large philodendron leaf. This seems just right. He puffs up his throat and adds his own call to the chorus of poison frogs in the area.

A loud chirp sounds behind him. It is an older frog telling him that this place is taken. Strawberry Frog answers but does not move. The old frog jumps on Strawberry Frog and they wrestle, chirping back and forth. Strawberry Frog is younger and stronger and the old frog gives in. He will have to find another spot. Strawberry Frog has won a territory!

"Eeh-eeh-eeh-eeh-eeh," he calls from his new calling spot.

Soon after, a female poison frog hops by on the forest floor and hears Strawberry Frog's call. Curious, the female climbs onto the philodendron leaf. Strawberry Frog chirps to the female poison frog. Then, knowing that she will follow, he turns around and hops away.

Strawberry Frog leads his new mate to a place that seems to him good for egg-laying. She looks it over, but the spot is not right for her. The two strawberry frogs hop away. Just in time! A passing coati, looking for insects to eat, starts digging right there with his sharp claws.

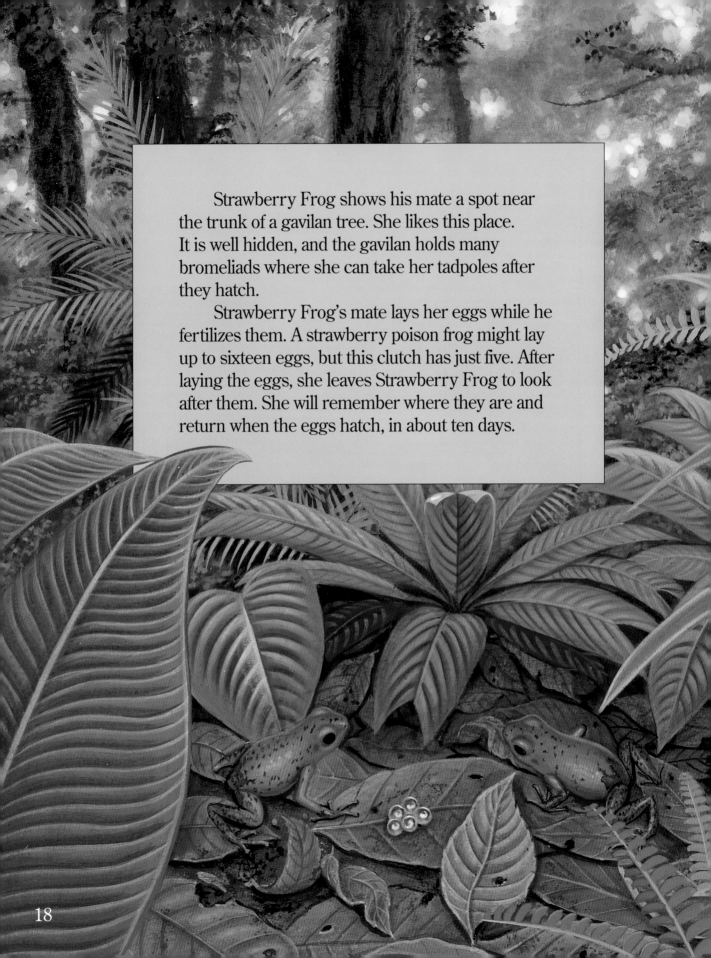

Strawberry Frog shows his mate a spot near the trunk of a gavilan tree. She likes this place. It is well hidden, and the gavilan holds many bromeliads where she can take her tadpoles after they hatch.

Strawberry Frog's mate lays her eggs while he fertilizes them. A strawberry poison frog might lay up to sixteen eggs, but this clutch has just five. After laying the eggs, she leaves Strawberry Frog to look after them. She will remember where they are and return when the eggs hatch, in about ten days.

Strawberry Frog warns other frogs away and keeps the eggs wet with liquid from his body. As he is guarding the eggs one afternoon, a young speckled racer slithers by.

The young racer has not learned that a bright-colored frog means poison. It grabs Strawberry Frog in its mouth. Quickly it spits out the bad-tasting creature and slides away, foaming at the mouth. This snake will not snap up a bright red frog the next time it sees one! Strawberry Frog, with one or two bite marks, hops back to care for the eggs.

The eggs begin to hatch and Strawberry Frog's mate returns. She backs in among the tadpoles, and one of them wriggles onto her back. Carrying the tadpole, she starts up the gavilan tree.

In the canopy, she finds a bromeliad and slides backward into its pool. The tadpole soon slips off her back into the water and begins to swim. Mother strawberry frog heads down the tree to get another tadpole.

23

On the mother frog's next trip up the tree she sees a laughing falcon tearing a bromeliad apart with its sharp beak, looking for food. Luckily, it is not the bromeliad where she left her first tadpole. She will put each one in a different bromeliad to make sure they have a better chance to survive. She remembers where she puts each of the tadpoles and comes every few days for the next three months to lay food eggs for them to eat.

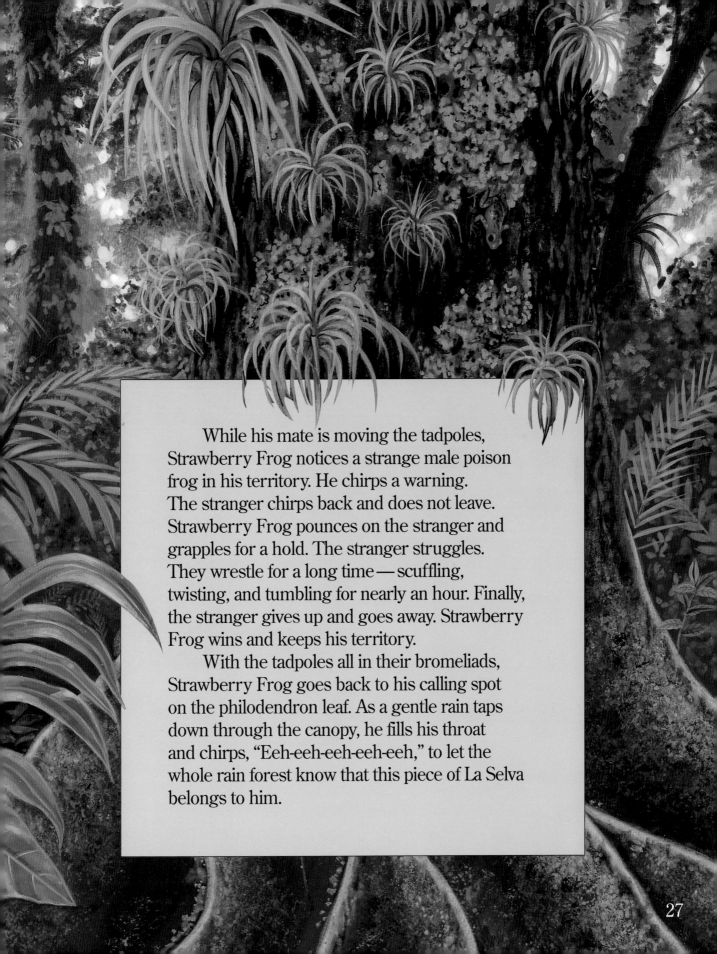

While his mate is moving the tadpoles, Strawberry Frog notices a strange male poison frog in his territory. He chirps a warning. The stranger chirps back and does not leave. Strawberry Frog pounces on the stranger and grapples for a hold. The stranger struggles. They wrestle for a long time — scuffling, twisting, and tumbling for nearly an hour. Finally, the stranger gives up and goes away. Strawberry Frog wins and keeps his territory.

With the tadpoles all in their bromeliads, Strawberry Frog goes back to his calling spot on the philodendron leaf. As a gentle rain taps down through the canopy, he fills his throat and chirps, "Eeh-eeh-eeh-eeh-eeh," to let the whole rain forest know that this piece of La Selva belongs to him.

La Selva, Costa Rica

La Selva is a private reserve that links to a large national park running from the Atlantic lowlands to the top of Volcan Barva and surrounding parts of Braulio Carillo National Park. The whole country of Costa Rica lies in the tropics—a warm, green belt that runs around the Equator.

About La Selva Rain Forest

La Selva, which means "the jungle" in Spanish, is a biological research station owned and operated by the Organization for Tropical Studies. It is a valuable biological station because it covers both very low and very high ground, and is all that is left of the huge evergreen forests that covered much of the Americas in the time of the dinosaurs—140 million years ago. It is home to over 850 kinds of birds, 376 kinds of reptiles and amphibians, and 205 types of mammals. There are so many insects that nobody has ever counted them all, and it has more plant species than in all of Europe put together.

Strawberry poison frogs live mostly in the dark world of the forest floor. Because of the toxins—or poisons—in their skins, most predators avoid them. Farther south in Colombia, South America, natives have used three other species of poison frogs to poison their hunting darts. They rub the darts on the skins of poison frogs to make the darts deadly. Nowadays, scientists study poison frogs as well as rare plants for clues that might give us valuable medicines.

The male poison frog's territory is small, usually only two or three meters, although he will go outside of that area to find food. The female travels more widely to go into the canopy to find bromeliads for her tadpoles.

Bromeliads are epiphytes, a kind of plant that grows on tree trunks, branches, or other plants to get closer to the sunlight. Epiphytes are sometimes called "air plants," because they have no roots in the soil and seem to live on air. They in fact get their food from plant and insect matter that collects in the water pools at the base of their leaves.

The biggest threat to strawberry poison frogs, and all rain forest species, is loss of habitat. Rain forest trees are cut for lumber. People clear rain forest land for farms and plantations. Once a rain forest is cut down, it can never grow back, and most all the creatures that lived there disappear. The Costa Rican government and many other people throughout the world are trying to find ways to preserve the rain forest. One way is setting up tree farms just for lumber, so loggers will not harvest rain forest trees. This is a good example of how people can earn a living and also save the rain forest.

Glossary

▲ *Blue morpho butterfly on philodendron leaf*

▲ *Green macaw*

▲ *Paraponera ant*

▲ *Broad-billed motmot*

▲ *Keel-billed toucan*

▲ *Passion-vine butterfly*

▲ *Bromeliad*

▲ *Olive tanager*

▲ *Strawberry poison frog*

▲ *Chestnut-backed antbird*

▲ *Orchids*

▲ *White bats*

▲ *Golden beetle*

▲ *White-faced capuchin monkey*

▲ *Cacique*

▲ *Heliconia caribaea*

▲ *Rufous-tailed hummingbird*

▲ *Cecropia*

▲ *Howler monkey*

▲ *Sierra palms*

▲ *Coati mundi*

▲ *Laughing falcon*

▲ *Speckled racer*

▲ *False-leaf katydid*

▲ *Leaf-cutter ants*

▲ *Three-toed sloth*

▲ *Red-kneed tarantula*